COAL
MINER'S

WRITERS' VOICES
SIGNAL HILL

ATTENTION READERS: We would like to hear what
you think about our books. Please send your comments
or suggestions to:

Signal Hill Publications
P.O. Box 131
Syracuse, NY 13210-0131

• • •

Selection: From COAL MINER'S DAUGHTER by
Loretta Lynn with George Vecsey. © 1976 by Loretta Lynn.
Reprinted by permission of Contemporary Books, Inc.

SIGNAL HILL

Additional material
© 1990 Signal Hill Publications
A publishing imprint of Laubach Literacy International

10 9 8 7 6 5 4 3 2

ISBN 0-929631-11-0

First printing: April 1990

The words 'Writers' Voices' are a trademark of
Signal Hill Publications.

Cover designed by Paul Davis Studio
Interior designed by Barbara Huntley

Signal Hill is a not-for-profit publisher. The proceeds
from the sale of this book go to support the national and
international programs of Laubach Literacy International.

PRINTED WITH
SOY INK

This book was printed on 100% recycled paper
which contains 50% post-consumer waste.

Acknowledgments

We gratefully acknowledge the generous support of the following foundations and corporations that made the publication of WRITERS' VOICES and NEW WRITERS' VOICES possible: The Vincent Astor Foundation; Booth Ferris Foundation; Exxon Corporation; James Money Management, Inc.; Scripps Howard Foundation; Uris Brothers Foundation, Inc.; The H.W. Wilson Foundation; and Weil, Gotshal & Manges Foundation Inc.

This book could not have been realized without the kind and generous cooperation of the author, Loretta Lynn, and her publisher, Contemporary Books, Inc.

We deeply appreciate the contributions of the following suppliers: Cam Steel Die Rule Works Inc. (steel cutting die for display); Canadian Pacific Forest Products Ltd. (text stock); Creative Graphics, Inc. (text typesetting); Horizon Paper Co., Inc. (cover stock); Martin/Friess Communications (display header); Mergenthaler Container (corrugated display); Phototype Color Graphics (cover color separations); and Ringier America Dresden Division (cover and text printing and binding).

Our thanks to Paul Davis Studio and Myrna Davis, Paul Davis, and Jeanine Esposito, for the inspired design of the covers of WRITERS' VOICES. Thanks also to Barbara Huntley for her sensitive attention to the interior design of this series.

CONTENTS

ABOUT *WRITERS' VOICES* ♩

"I want to read what others do—what I see people reading in libraries, on the subway, and at home."

> Mamie Moore, a literacy student,
> Brooklyn, New York

Writer's Voices is our response to Mamie Moore's wish:

- the wish to step forward into the reading community,
- the wish to have access to new information,
- the wish to read to her grandchildren,
- the wish to read for the joy of reading.

NOTE TO THE READER ♪:

"What we are familiar with, we cease to see. The writer shakes up the familiar scene, and, as if by magic, we see a new meaning in it."   Anaïs Nin

Writers' Voices invites you to discover new meaning. One way to discover new meaning is to learn something new. Another is to see in a new way something you already know.

Writers' Voices is a series of books. Each book contains selections from one or more writers' work. We chose the selections because the writers' voices can be clearly heard. Also, they deal with experiences that are interesting to think about and discuss.

If you are a new reader, you may want to have a selection read aloud to you, perhaps more than once. This will free you to enjoy the piece, to hear the language used, and to think about its meaning. Even if you are a more experienced reader, you may en-

7

joy hearing the selection read aloud before reading it silently to yourself.

Each selection is set in a framework to expand your understanding of the selection. The framework includes a chapter that tells about the writer's life.

You may also find chapters about the characters, the plot, and when or where the story took place. These will help you begin thinking about the selection. They will also help you understand what may be unfamiliar to you.

We encourage you to read *actively*. An active reader does many things—while reading, and before and after reading—that help him or her better understand and enjoy a book. Here are some suggestions of things you can do:

Before Reading

• Read the front and back covers of the book, and look at the cover illustration. Ask yourself what you expect the book to be about, based on this information.
• Think about why you want to read this

book. What do you want to discover, and what questions do you hope will be answered?

• Look at the contents page. Decide which chapters you want to read and in what order you want to read them.

During Reading

• Try to stay with the rhythm of the language. If you find any words or sentences you don't understand, keep reading to see if the meaning becomes clear. If it doesn't, go back and reread the difficult part or discuss it with others.

• Try to put yourself into the story.

• Ask yourself questions as you read. For example: Do I believe this story or this character? Why?

After Reading

• Ask yourself if the story makes you see any of your own experiences in a new way.

• Ask yourself if the story has given you any new information.

• Keep a journal in which you can write down your thoughts about what you have read, and save new words you have learned.

• Look over the questions at the end of the book. They are meant to help you discover more about what you have read and how it relates to you—as a person, as a reader, and as a writer. Try those questions that seem most interesting to you.

• Talk about what you have read with other readers.

Good writing should make you think after you put the book down. Whether you are a beginning reader, a more experienced reader, or a teacher of reading, we encourage you to take time to think about these books and to discuss your thoughts with others. If you want to read more books by the author of the selections, you can go to your bookstore or library to find them.

When you are finished with the book, we hope you will write to our editors about your reactions. We want to know your thoughts about our books, and what they have meant to you.

ABOUT THE SELECTIONS FROM
COAL MINER'S DAUGHTER ♪

In 1976, Loretta Lynn published a book that told her life story. She called it *Coal Miner's Daughter,* which is also the title of one of her songs. It is also the title of the movie based on the book.

Loretta Lynn is one of the most famous and successful country singers of our time. Yet she began life in a poor family in the mountains of eastern Kentucky. She had little education and no formal training in music.

She married Doo Lynn when she was 13 years old, and they moved to Washington state. Loretta had four babies by the time she was 18. She didn't begin her singing career until she was 24 years old.

To write her book, Loretta worked with a writer, George Vecsey. Loretta talked into a tape recorder, telling the story of her life. Vecsey then took this information and put it together to make the book.

In the selections from *Coal Miner's Daughter*, you will read about Loretta's childhood, her parents, her husband, and her singing career. She also has included many of her opinions about things that have happened to her.

Perhaps you will recognize feelings or experiences you have in common with Loretta Lynn. Perhaps you will want to recall what you know about her and see if her life story, as she tells it, is what you expected.

A TIMELINE FOR LORETTA LYNN ♩.

1935   born in Butcher Hollow, Kentucky

1948   married

1960   started singing professionally

1960   made first recording

1962   signed lifetime record contract

1966   bought mansion and land at Hurricane Mills, Tennessee

1969   wrote the song *Coal Miner's Daughter*

1972   named Entertainer of the Year

1976   wrote the book *Coal Miner's Daughter*

1980   named Entertainer of the Decade
the movie, *Coal Miner's Daughter*, is released

MAP OF PLACES MENTIONED
IN THE SELECTIONS

Custer, WASHINGTON

Nashville, TENNESSEE

Butcher Hollow,
KENTUCKY

Los Angeles,
CALIFORNIA

N

SELECTED FROM
COAL MINER'S DAUGHTER
LORETTA LYNN with George Vecsey

About Me and This Book ♫

I bloodied my husband's nose the other night.
I didn't know I was doing it—I just woke up
at three in the morning, and Doolittle was
holding a towel to his nose. He told me I sat
straight up, in my sleep, yelling, "Do you
see this ring? Do you see this ring?" And I
was a-throwing my hands around until my
fingers dug into his nose.

"Loretta, what in the world were you
talking about?" Doo asked me.

I said I was dreaming about some old guy
that tried to make a date with me when I first
started singing. I didn't have no ring at the
time—we were too poor for that kind of
stuff—but now in my dream I was showing
that old buzzard I had a ring.

What does it mean when you carry on in
your sleep like that? Somebody said it

means you've got something on your mind. I said, "I *know* that." I ain't got much education, but I got some sense.

To me, this talking is almost like I've got things inside me that never came out before. Usually, when something is bothering me, I write a song that tells my feelings, like: "Don't Come Home A-Drinkin' (with Lovin' on Your Mind)." That's really about me and my marriage.

I've still got things inside me—sad things, happy things—that people don't know about. I've had so many changes in my life, and I feel like there's more to come.

People know the basic facts about me, how I was married when I wasn't quite fourteen and had four babies by the time I was eighteen. Sometimes my husband tells me, "I raised you the way I wanted you to be." And it's true. I went from Daddy to Doo, and there's always been a man telling me what to do.

I was just a kid—didn't know nothing—picking strawberries in the fields with my babies on a blanket, under an umbrella. I'd change a few diapers, my fingers all rough and dirty, give 'em a few bottles, and go back to picking. So when I sing those country songs about women struggling to keep things going, you could say I've been there.

Now I've got this huge ranch in Tennessee, and I've been on the cover of *Newsweek* magazine, and I was the first woman ever named "Entertainer of the Year" in country music. I also got honorable mention in the Gallup Poll as one of the "most admired women" in the United States. Lordy, I even got to meet Gregory Peck!

But some of my friends, who know me best, say they wouldn't trade places with me for a million dollars because of the pace I lead. I'm still a-traveling nearly two hundred nights a year to meet my fans who've given me everything I've got. In one way, I'm still working as hard as when I was working in the fields. But I'd have to admit, the stakes are higher.

When I first came to Nashville, people called us "hillbilly singers" and hardly gave country music any respect. We lived in old cars and dirty hotels, and we ate when we could. Now country music is a big business.

When we started on this book, me and Doolittle talked it over about how much we should tell about ourselves. Suppose I don't like the way he acts when he's drinking. Or suppose Doo thinks I'm meaner than a snake. Should we tell our troubles to other people in a book?

Well, Doo leaned back in his chair and thought about it for a minute. Then he said, "Hell's fire, Loretta, just tell the story the way it happened. I've always said you should never try to cover up things. Look, we're not perfect. Let's not pretend we are."

Somebody said I should write all these memories down. But it ain't like writing a song. I mean, when I get a title for a song, I scribble it down on a napkin or an old paper bag, anything that's handy. Then when I get back to my room, I just start singing those words until I've got me a song.

People say I can't read or write because I've only got about a fourth-grade education. But I can read and write some. I'm not pretending I know how to write a book—not even a book about me. I'm too nervous to even sit in front of a tape recorder for long. I've always been full of nervous energy, and I've gotten used to clowning around onstage, and offstage, too.

But I'm not really as happy as I seem. I've known a lot of sad times in my life that don't square with that lady you see clowning up on the stage. You get used to sadness, growing up in the mountains, I guess. I was given up to die when I was a baby. I came close to drowning near my ranch a few years ago—I never told nobody about that until now. And the doctors told me my heart stopped on the operating table when I had chest surgery in 1972. Ever since then, I've wanted to tell my life story.

The way I did it was this: the writers have always been really nice to me, and I've always enjoyed sitting and talking to 'em. But we finally got together with this one writer who used to live in Kentucky, name of George. He knows my part of the country real well; he's visited the coal mines, and he's been up to the hollers, so he speaks my language. Now for the past year he's been traveling with me and Doolittle. I've taken him to Butcher Holler and introduced him to my Uncle Corman. I've taken him to the ranch and shown him all my scrapbooks. He's met my best friends.

You can bet your last scrip penny I checked out every word before they sent it to the book company. And if I didn't think it was true, out it went.

The first thing I insisted was that it sound like me. When all those city folks try to fix up my talking, all they do is mess me up. Like the way I pronounce the word "holler." That's our word for the low space between two mountains. City people pronounce it "hollow" but that ain't the way I pronounce it. This is *my* book. Instead of using Webster's Dictionary, we're using Webb's Dictionary—Webb was my maiden name.

So when you're reading this book, just try to picture me up on stage, singing my songs and clowning around, and try to hear me saying "Butcher Holler." Then you'll know it's me.

Butcher Holler ♪

Most people know that much about me, because those are the first words of my biggest song. I open my show with it because I know people are gonna request it until I sing it. I wrote it myself, nine verses, and it broke my heart when I had to cut three verses out because it was too long. I could have written a thousand more verses, I've got so many memories of Butcher Holler.

To me, that place is the most important part of my life. My fans and writers are always making a big deal about me acting natural, right from the country. That's because I come from Butcher Holler, Kentucky, and I ain't never forgot it.

I'm always making Butcher Holler sound

like the most backward part of the United States—and I think maybe it is. I've traveled all over this country, down South and out West, and I ain't never seen anything like it. And I ain't making fun of it, because I'm the most backward person you ever saw. I never knew where babies came from until it happened to me.

Holler people are just different from anybody else. They live high up in the hills, one day at a time. There's probably a few who don't know who the president is, and there have been times when they were better off that way. Maybe things are changing now, with television and better roads and stuff, but I've got relatives living up in Butcher Holler who have never been further than Paintsville, ten miles away, in their lives. They're really beautiful people in their own way.

Let me explain where Butcher Holler is. You take any place in the United States today, and they've got an interstate highway, right? Well, you get on one of them interstates and drive to Huntington, West Virginia, which is already in pretty hilly country—

but you ain't seen nothing yet. You get off Interstate 64 and head south along Highway 23 into Kentucky. That's a good three-lane highway going past some nice farms and factories and mobile homes. You drive for about an hour and a half until you get to Paintsville, which has around 4,000 people.

Paintsville may not look too big to outsiders, but in Johnson County it's the biggest thing going. That's the first place I ever saw a toilet with running water, just before I got married. I went into the bus station to go to the bathroom, but when I sat down on the seat, the toilet flushed automatically. I got so scared I was gonna get flushed down, I ran out of there and waited until we found a good old outhouse.

When I was a little girl, my big city was Van Lear, which was five miles away, a coal camp for the Consolidated Coal Company, with rows of wooden houses they rented to the miners. There must have been 10,000 people living around Van Lear in the good times. The company had a post office and company stores where you paid for your things in scrip. If you went into debt, you owed your soul to the company store, just like the song says. The company also had a recreation hall where they showed movies. People make coal camps sound like slavery, but in a lot of ways it was the best thing ever happened to people—as long as the coal kept running.

My home was maybe four miles further up the mountains from Van Lear. The road was paved up to the mines, then it was topped with just coal slag—"red dog," we called it. That ran from the upper company store to the one-room schoolhouse. Then there was just a dirt path leading alongside the creek, in the narrow space between two ridges.

As you walked up the holler, the path got steeper and steeper, with trees growing on both sides of you. You had this feeling of being all wrapped up in the trees and hills, real secure-like. If you'd stop walking and just listen, you could hear a couple of kids playing outside, or maybe some birds in the trees. I used to love going out-of-doors at night and listening to the whippoorwills. Maybe it was the Cherokee in me, but I loved being outside. In the summertime, we'd hold lightning bugs (that's our word for fireflies) on our fingers and pretend they were diamond rings. Or we'd just sit there in the holler, and it would be perfectly quiet.

Holler kids were so bashful that they'd run and hide if they had company coming. I was still bashful after I was married and didn't make friends easily. The only way my husband could get me out of it was to tell me I was ignorant. See, he'd traveled outside the mountains. He'd been around.

My folks don't make a big fuss over me in Butcher Holler. They knew me when I was wearing flour sacks, so I ain't no big deal to them. I can go back there and we'll talk just the same way we always did—tell snake stories and ghost stories, believing about half of it.

We didn't even have cars when I was

living there. When I was born, there was no sense in going to the hospital. We couldn't afford it anyway, not with the Depression going on. So we had this old woman, Old Aunt Harriet, around eighty years old, come to deliver me. She was almost blind, Mommy said, and she had to feel with her fingers where to cut the cord. Daddy had to sell our milk cow, Old Goldy, to pay thirty-five dollars to Old Aunt Harriet so she'd stay two weeks with Mommy.

After I was born, Mommy put me in the crib in the corner. We just had this one-room cabin they made from logs, with the cracks filled with moss and clay. The wind used to whistle in so bad, Mommy would paper the walls with pages from her Sears and Roebuck catalog and movie magazines. Mommy never went to the movies, but she always liked pictures of Loretta Young and Claudette Colbert. Right over my crib she pasted pictures of them two stars. That's how I got my name. Lots of times I wonder if I would have made it in country music if I was named Claudette.

Daddy

Even though he died before I ever got started singing, in 1959, I feel like Daddy's been the most important person in my life. I'm very close to Mommy, too, and though Doolittle has just about raised me since I was a girl, I had almost fourteen years of Daddy giving me love and security, the way a daddy should. He'd sit and hold me on his lap while he rocked by the fireplace. I think Daddy is the main reason why I always had respect for myself when times got rough between me and Doolittle—I knew my Daddy loved me.

We've got some pictures of Daddy, and he's usually got this straight face on him, not much emotion. Mountain people are like that. It's hard to read 'em if you don't know 'em. He was real shy, not like people from the coal camps who are used to talking with each other. But Butcher Holler was his kind of world. There, he was the greatest man you ever saw. He could fix anything with those wiry arms of his. He could hammer up a well box, or a fence for the hog, or a new outhouse. You had to do things for yourself in the hollers or you'd die.

Daddy's name was Melvin—Melvin Webb—but everybody called him "Ted." His daddy and mommy lived in Butcher Holler; she was a Butcher, from the first family that settled up there. One of Daddy's grandmothers was a full-blooded Cherokee squaw, and it's the same on my mother's side. So that means I'm one-quarter Cherokee— and proud of it. Other kids called me "half-breed" when I was a kid, but it didn't bother me. Being Indian was no big deal one way or the other. A lot of blood was mixed up in the hollers, if the truth be known. I was always proud of being Indian—and I've gotten more proud as the years go on.

Daddy didn't go to school much, but he could read and write some. He worked out-of-doors when he was young, farming and stuff. When he was about twenty, he met Mommy at the little church in the holler. They courted for around two years and then got married. They built their own little one-room wood cabin at the end of the holler. She would hold the boards and he would drive in the nails. Right after the Depression started, they began having kids—eight of them, four boys and four girls, in the next sixteen years. I was next to the oldest.

Daddy couldn't get much work during the Depression, and we didn't have money. I remember one Christmas when Daddy had only thirty-six cents for four children. Somehow, he managed to buy a little something for each of us down at the general store. He gave me a little plastic doll about three inches high, and I loved that like it was my own baby.

Daddy was more easygoing than Mommy. She did most of the correcting in the family. The only time Daddy would get mad was when someone would smart off at Mommy. Then he'd move right in there and settle it. He wasn't one of those men that's gone half the time either—he didn't have no bad habits. He was always teasing Mommy, but in a nice way. If she got mad about something, he'd laugh and say, "The Squaw's on the warpath tonight." I never forgot that line, and I wrote a song about it when I got older. But you know—the nice way he treated her gave me ideas about the way I wanted to be treated. I still feel there's better ways to handle a woman than whipping her into line. And I make that point clear in my songs, in case you hadn't noticed.

When the Depression got better, Daddy saved enough money to buy a house with four rooms in it. It was down the holler, next to his folks, in a big, broad clearing. We had a spring behind the house for fresh water and a well in front. We had a new outhouse in the back. In the winter, you'd wait too long because you didn't want to go outside in the cold. And then you'd have to run through the snow, hoping you'd make it to the outhouse. We still didn't have electricity, and our bunch of kids still had to sleep on pallets in the living room at night. But we had four rooms instead of one, and we really thought we'd arrived.

Finally, the mines got to working again,

and Daddy decided to support his family as a coal miner. He never worked in the mines before, and it must have taken a lot of nerve to go into that terrible dark hole. But Daddy did it for us.

He worked at Consolidated Number Five, right down the holler. The seam of coal was only three feet high, and you can bet they didn't bother cutting the rock to give the men a place to stand up. That meant the miners had to crawl on their hands and knees and work on their sides or lying on their backs. Some of the miners wore knee pads, like the basketball players wear, but Daddy found that they raised him up so high that his back rubbed against the roof as he crawled into the mine. So he would come home every night with his knees all cut and sore, and he'd soak them in hot water before he could go to sleep. But the next morning he'd be out working in the garden again, until it was time to go to the mine.

Daddy worked the night shift. He left home around four o'clock every afternoon and walked down the holler. We kids, we hardly said good-bye to him. But looking back, I can see the worried look on Mommy's face. She would keep busy with the kids all afternoon and evening. She had her hands full. But after we were in bed, she would sit by the kerosene lamp and read her Bible or an old Western book until she heard Daddy coming up the steps. They'd lie in bed talking, but I never heard him complain about the mines. Coal miners are funny that way. They don't like to get their wives upset. I feel real proud of Daddy for working in the mines. He kept his family alive by breaking his own body down. That's the only way to look at it.

After he worked in the mines for a few years, he had trouble breathing. The doctors used to say that a miner was "nervous" or that he smoked too much. They didn't know about black lung in those days. Black lung is what you get when you breathe in too much coal dust. It never leaves your lungs—just stays there and clogs up your breathing, puts extra strain on your heart.

They used to tell the miners that coal dust was good for you, that it helped ward off colds. Or they'd tell a miner he would get sicker from dirty sheets than from working in a coal mine—lots of stupid things, but nobody knew any better then.

Sometimes Daddy didn't take a bath before he came home, and all you could see was the whites of his eyes. Well, if that coal dust could stick to his face like that, it must have gotten into his lungs, too. But it wasn't until some time after Daddy died that the miners just plumb refused to work unless the government paid them benefits. And all the time, England and other European countries was paying off their miners with black lung. I've got relatives collecting black lung benefits today, but it came too late for Daddy. He got laid off when he couldn't work fast anymore. They just said, "Take your shovel and go home." No pension, no benefits, just "go home." This was after I moved away, but Mommy wrote me a letter. They tried running a grocery store, but that didn't work out because some people came down to get groceries but didn't pay him. He left the world owing nobody anything, but a lot of people owed him.

I remember after World War II, Daddy saving up enough money for a battery-operated Philco radio. I'll never forget him pulling that radio up the holler on his sled and putting it in the corner of the living room, so proud of himself. It was the first radio we ever owned. I was eleven years old. Daddy didn't let us run it all the time because he wanted to save the batteries for Saturday night, when he was off from work. He would sit there by the grate, where it was warm, and turn on Lowell Thomas and the news. I still hear that great deep voice of Lowell Thomas today, and it makes me think of Daddy. Then we'd get our favorite radio program of all—The Grand Ole Opry, direct from Nashville, Tennessee.

I can't say that I had big dreams of being a star at the Opry. It was another world to me. All I knew was Butcher Holler—didn't have no dreams that I knew about. But I'd curl up by Daddy and the radio and fall asleep, and on Sunday morning I'd find the radio still turned on, nothing playing, just some crackling noises. But inside my head I could still hear that music.

Mommy

To me, my mother always was the most beautiful woman in the world. A redheaded Irish girl was her mother and a half Cherokee was her father. So Mommy's one-quarter Cherokee, with blue eyes and coal black hair that's just now turning gray. Her skin gets dark if she just works in the garden for an hour. Her eyes look Irish, but her cheekbones look Indian. I always wanted to be as beautiful as Mommy, but I never made it. She and I have the same nose, but I've got these buck teeth that I've always hated.

After Mommy got married, she used her Indian ways to raise us. She had her first seven kids at home, with an old midwife coming in to help. The last one, she went down to Paintsville Hospital to have. She figured she earned that. After Mommy had me, she was out setting onions on the hill only three days later. Mommy did everything the way they do it now—more natural. They get you up on your feet the first day now, and they let you go home after three days. Mommy was just ahead of her time. All eight children are alive today—so she must have been doing something right.

Whatever went wrong up on our holler, Mommy would take care of it. For burns, she'd make a salve of castor oil, flour, and sulphur. She'd cook it all together, then rub it on the wound and it would heal real fast. When you got a cold, Mommy would make a poultice from mustard seeds and rub it on your chest. It would take the cold right out of you. But it was so hot and smelly, us kids would swear we'd rather have the cold than the poultice.

School Days ♪

You've got to be honest about yourself, and I'll be the first to admit I don't have too much education.

For a long time, I never got my driver's license because I was scared of taking reading tests.

I write down the words to my songs, and I can read the Bible pretty well. I've also read some history books about my Indians to find out what the white man did.

I *ought* to be able to read a little, because Mommy made sure all us kids walked two miles down the holler to the one-room schoolhouse. There's a big difference between holler kids and coal-camp kids. The kids in Van Lear went to a regular school with one teacher for each grade, but we only had one teacher for all eight grades. Usually, we had six or seven different teachers a year. I guess they didn't get paid too good—or else we scared off those teachers who didn't know how to handle us.

When I got bigger, I got the job of walking to school early and starting the fire in the potbellied stove. I'd get paid a dollar a month for that. I also cleaned erasers and did little jobs. I was real proud because I was earning money and helping the teacher. I could add four and four and I could read the primer—"There goes Alice. Here comes Spot." So I'd start teaching the younger ones. We only had a few books and when we got new workbooks one year, we thought we were really something. I went to school clear through the eighth grade. I liked it so much I even repeated the eighth grade. Don't forget, there wasn't any ninth grade. But the way education used to be in one-room schoolhouses is about like fourth grade in a regular school.

Another reason I liked school was because we had this program on Friday where the kids performed. Mommy made me a ruffled, red crepe-paper dress, and I wore it until it fell apart. And I'd get up in front of the class and sing for as long as they let me.

Sometimes people ask me what kind of music we sang back in eastern Kentucky in those days. Well, it was our own music. I know there's some kind of history to mountain music—like it came from Ireland or England or Scotland and we kept up the tradition, hidden off in the mountains. I know there are folk musicians who come down to the mountains to make tape recordings of the old people singing the old hymns and stuff. But I couldn't honestly say if we had that kind of music.

Most of our songs told a story. You could tell me that's the old-fashioned way people had of telling news, before newspapers and radio. All I know is, most country songs are ballads. Like we'd sing true songs about somebody getting killed. Mommy taught me a song called "The Great Titanic" and she taught me how to make motions with my hands to help in telling the story. Like when the ship went down, I'd curve my hands downward.

Most of our songs we learned from our friends and our family. We didn't sing too much stuff from the radio when I was little because, like I said before, we didn't have a radio until I was eleven. The first song I remember on the radio was "I'm Walking the Floor over You," with Ernest Tubb singing. Nowadays, I can stand right on the stage and watch my friend Ernest Tubb singing that same song. Thrilled? That ain't the word for it.

Nowadays, people learn their songs from the radio or records. You go up to the mountains and the kids all know the top country songs, even rock 'n' roll. But they don't know the old songs anymore.

Beginner's Luck ♫

As you can tell, I've always liked to sing. But the singing career was Doolittle's idea. I was sitting home on our anniversary. I was already twenty-four years old. My oldest girl was ten. I was embroidering pheasants and bird dogs. Doolittle had something on his mind. I could tell because his face gets kind of drawn-in when he's thinking. He had got me this seventeen-dollar Harmony guitar at Sears and Roebuck for my eighteenth birthday, and I had started to learn to play the thing. This was the first guitar I ever owned— before, all I'd ever done was hold my brother's guitar sometimes. Now a few years later, Doo said I had a good voice and he wanted me to sing. What did I think? Well, I was surprised. Stunned, you could say. I didn't know Doolittle thought that much about my singing. I was proud to be noticed, to tell you the truth, so I went right to work on it. When the kids were in school or asleep at night, I'd sit in my front room, learning how to play the guitar better. I never took no lessons or nothing—I just played. After a while, I got where I could play a pretty good tune on it. First I was singing Kitty Wells's songs on it, but after a while I started making up my own.

I think I practiced about two months on that guitar. Then Doolittle started telling me I had to sing in public. It was a big step, because I didn't think I was ready to face an audience. I was so bashful that if strangers even talked to me I'd turn away, so I sure didn't want to go singing in public. But he said it was a chance for us to make some extra money, so I kept practicing. He said I could do it, and he said he'd set me up at some club. So I did it—because he said I could. He made all the decisions in those days.

Now that's what I mean when I say my husband is responsible for my career. It wasn't my idea: he told me I could do it. I'd still be a housewife today if he didn't bring that guitar home and then encourage me to be a singer.

* * *

Doo finally hooked Loretta up with the Penn Brothers, who had a radio show and played local clubs. They paid her $5 a performance and Loretta thought she was a millionaire. Soon, Loretta had her own group that played in local taverns and at fairs.

Her big break came when she won the amateur night contest on the Buck Owens television show. A wealthy man named Norm Burley saw the show. He gave Loretta and Doo the money to have a record made of "I'm a Honky Tonk Girl."

An Honest-to-Goodness Record ♫

We didn't have any studio or a band so we went to these studios in Los Angeles. I'd sit outside and wait for Doo to come out. Each time he'd get this sad look on his face and I figured, "we can't even *pay* to get me on a record. Nobody will even take our money." But then Doo went up to this studio where Speedy West worked. He was well known in country music. Somehow they agreed to let me make my record.

I went inside to this little studio about half the size of a motel room. But I saw these men and machines and a few musicians, and I got all scared. I still didn't know about notes or anything, but I showed 'em the words and hummed the tune and they started to fiddle around. After I sang a few lines, Speedy West said, "Hey, let's hold it up a few hours and get a few more pickers.''

What he did, really, was to get better pickers. He must of heard something he liked, because he brought in some good musicians from around town and they picked up on my song real well. By the end of the day we had both sides recorded—''Whispering Sea'' was the other side. And a few weeks later they sent us a shipment of records with the Zero label.

The record was fine, but we were pitiful. We didn't know anything about releasing a record, but we tried our best. Doolittle had a hobby of photography at the time, so he made up a picture of me. We mailed out 3,500 copies of the record and my picture and sent them to every radio station we could find. We had a list of all the country stations—I don't know how we got that. We even wrote a little bit about my life.

We'd call up the disc jockeys and ask 'em to play the record, and most of 'em did. Those boys have always been on our side. But we couldn't get the records to the stores fast enough. Someone would hear the record on the jukebox or the radio, then go into a store and ask to buy it—and the owner wouldn't have it. It was a big mess, but we really tried to get those records out. And all that time, Doolittle was still working at his full-time auto-mechanic's job in the garage, paying our bills and keeping us alive.

One day in the summer, our steel-guitar man came over to the house and said, "Hey, your record is on the charts." We were so stupid we didn't know what the charts meant. But it meant we were in the top ten in some places, based on jukebox plays. The July 25, 1960 *Billboard* listed us as number fourteen in the national country music charts.

So we took off in our old Mercury, trying to promote the record. We went down the West Coast, too poor to stay in motels, sleeping in the car and eating baloney and cheese sandwiches. To this day I can't stand any sandwiches for that reason. I ate too many of 'em when I was young. I only had one good dress. When we were driving, I'd just wear jeans or something. We had this list of radio stations and we'd keep turning the dial as we drove. When we got near a station, I'd hop in the back of the car and change into my dress. Then we'd go inside the radio station.

We didn't care if it was a 500-watt local station or a 50,000-watt clear channel station, we'd hit 'em all. The little stations were better for us. When you're little, you appreciate someone else who's little. I was just a nobody. I'd walk into the station and introduce myself. That was hard at first, because I was so bashful. But those disc jockeys were nice to me everywhere. I looked like a kid—my hair was curly back in those days and Doolittle never let me wear any makeup.

I'd stay in those radio stations as long as they let me talk on the air—and there was Doolittle sitting out in the car, listening to me on the radio, getting burned up if I said something dumb. But you know something, I was starting to enjoy myself, meeting all those boys. It was more exciting then than it is now. Nowadays I never stop at country stations anymore because of our tight schedule. And besides, my bus wouldn't fit in the driveway. It's such a different deal now.

I remember going into a station in Tucson, Arizona, where the disc jockey was a little boy, same age as me, pimples on his face, greasy hair. He was so nice to me that we used to write letters back and forth until he got into singing, too. Waylon Jennings, that's who it was. One disc jockey who remembers me is Hugh Cherry. He was working an all-night show on KFOX in Long Beach, California. One evening I rang his buzzer and said to him, "A disc jockey in Seattle said if someone wants to get a hillbilly record to break in California, you are the man to see. Well, I've got one here, 'Honky Tonk Girl.' It's mine."

He played it and liked it. We told him we were distributing it ourselves to every disc jockey on our way to Nashville to get on the Grand Ole Opry. He couldn't believe it when I said Doo was waiting in the car. He said, "But honey, don't you know it takes three or four years to get on the Opry?'' I told him, ''Maybe so, but I can't wait that long.''

Well, we got to the Opry that same year, the year we started singing. And in that same year, I was listed right behind Jan Howard, Margie Bowes, and Connie Hall as ''Most Promising Girl Singer.'' The next time I saw Hugh Cherry he said, ''Well, you made it—lots sooner than I expected!''

Songwriter

People forget that I'm a songwriter. They think of me as just a lady up on the stage, with a band backing her up. Well, let me tell you, I've sat in my room all night, scratching out most of my songs, going all the way back to those sorry little songs I wrote back in Washington.

People say I can't read or write, but what about ''Coal Miner's Daughter?'' I wrote every line, just from things I remember from my childhood.

The way most of my songs got started

was I'd hear a good line or make one up.
When I get a good first line, I'll scribble it
down on a piece of paper, hotel stationery,
paper bag, or whatever, and slip it into my
purse. Usually I write my songs at night.
When I get 'em written down, I'm relaxed
and I go to sleep. In the morning, I finish
the song and try to find a tune for it, just
starting with the first line and humming to
myself. After I get the tune, I get somebody
else to write down the notes for me because
I still can't read music after all these years.
But I don't think many country musicians
are good at reading music. You go to one
of our recording sessions and somebody
will say, ''Hey, how about doing it this
way?'' And he'll rip off a few notes on the
guitar. And somebody else will say, ''Oh,
you mean like this?'' And he'll rip off a
few more notes. It's like they communicate
with their own music language. Those
studio musicians don't need written notes.

Most of my songs were from the woman's
point of view. In the old days, country music
was directed at the men—truck-driving songs,

easy women, cheating songs. I remember how excited I got back in 1952, the first time I heard Kitty Wells sing "It Wasn't God Who Made Honky-Tonk Angels." That was the women's answer to that Hank Thompson record called "The Wild Side of Life." See, Kitty was presenting the woman's point of view, which is different from the man's. And I always remembered that when I started writing songs.

What's Next? ♪♪

This is my life today, my "glamorous" life. Sometimes I ask myself, how long is this gonna go on? My twins are always asking, "Mommy, when are you going to stay home?" And my doctor tries to cut down my travel time because of my migraines and high blood pressure.

A lot of people say I'd really miss show business if I quit. Well, I'd miss some of it. But I never realized it would be like this when I started—all this traveling. Now it's the only life I know.

It's been almost fifteen years since me and Doolittle had what I'd call a normal life, if we ever were normal, that is. I sometimes wonder what it would be like if I stayed home. We argue like crazy when I stay home for a day or two. It's really kind of funny. I've worked all my life and now I'm in a spot where men tell me how to run my business, and when I go home other people tell me how to run my home.

But all that is changing. I'm not the bashful little girl I was fifteen years ago, when my only dream was a comfortable house for my family. In those days, if Doolittle disappeared for a day or two, I just accepted it. I got mad—but I accepted it. I'm different today. I refuse to be pushed around anymore.

I know how lucky I've been. I wouldn't have dared to ask God for all that He's given me. I'm just grateful for the benefits my family has enjoyed. I didn't do it. I couldn't have done it on my own. I thank God every day for what I have.

ABOUT LORETTA LYNN

Loretta Webb Lynn has been called the "Queen of Country Music." She is small and slender, standing 5′2″ tall, with long, brown hair. She has high cheekbones and sparkling blue eyes.

Loretta was born on April 14, 1935, in Butcher Hollow, a few miles from Van Lear, a coal-mining town in eastern Kentucky. Her parents were Clara and Melvin Webb. Loretta was the second of eight children. One of her sisters is the singer Crystal Gayle.

Loretta's family was very poor. Their house had no electricity, no running water, and no bathroom. In fact, the family didn't have much of anything except closeness and love. But, as Loretta says, "We didn't know we were poor because everybody else in Butcher Holler was as poor as we were."

In January 1948, when she was only 13 years old, Loretta married Oliver Vanetta Lynn, whom Loretta calls "Doo." Doo was seven years older than she was, and he had been a soldier in World War II. Doo bought Loretta her first party dress and her first restaurant meal, and took her to her first movie and on her first car ride.

After they got married, Loretta and Doo moved to the town of Custer, Washington, where he worked as a mechanic, a logger, and a bronco buster. To make money, she sometimes took in washing and picked strawberries with migrant workers.

Loretta began her singing career when she was 24 years old. One night she and Doo went to the local grange hall to hear some country music. Doo stood up and said that Loretta was a better country singer than anyone except Kitty Wells, the top country singer at the time. Loretta didn't sing that night, but she did appear on a local radio show a few days later.

In 1960, she made her first recording, "I'm a Honky Tonk Girl." That same year, Loretta appeared on the Grand Ole Opry radio show for 21 weeks. Loretta and Doo moved to Nashville.

Doo is Loretta's business manager, but he usually doesn't travel with her around the country. When their children were small, he stayed home and took care of them.

Loretta and Doo had six children. In the first four years after they were married, they had Betty Sue, Jack Benny, Carla, and Ernest Ray. In 1964, their twins, Peggy and Patsy, were born.

Loretta has always been a very active entertainer. In the 1960s and 1970s, she traveled nine or ten months a year and often gave two shows a night. These days, she doesn't go on the road quite as much. She travels in a custom-built bus with bunks for her band, and a special bedroom and dressing room for herself.

In 1966, Loretta and Doo bought a mansion and about 3,000 acres of land at Hurricane Mills, Tennessee, a small town near Nashville. They no longer live in the mansion, but the Loretta Lynn Dude Ranch is still there, as well as a museum of Loretta's life and career. Loretta and Doo now have their main home in Nashville, but they also own houses in Mexico and Hawaii.

The year 1972 was a big one for Loretta. She was named Entertainer of the Year (the first woman ever to get this award) and Best Female Vocalist by the Country Music Association. That same year, she and Conway Twitty received the award for Top Vocal Duo. They received the same award again many times in later years.

In 1984, Loretta Lynn lost her oldest son, Jack, who died in an accident while riding his horse. Loretta has called the year that followed "the worst year of my life."

Loretta Lynn has made more than 80 record albums. In 1980, she was named Artist of the Decade by the Academy of Country Music. She has had more charted singles than any other female artist, including 16 number one hits.

Loretta's book, *Coal Miner's Daughter*, was a best-seller, with more than a million copies in print. A 1980 movie was based on the book. It was a box-office hit. The movie starred Sissy Spacek and Tommy Lee Jones.

LORETTA LYNN'S GREATEST HITS

SONG TITLE	*YEAR*
I'm a Honky Tonk Girl	1960
Before I'm Over You	1962
Success	1962
The Other Woman	1963
Blue Kentucky Girl	1964
Wine Women and Song	1964
You Ain't Woman Enough (To Take My Man)	1965
Don't Come Home A-Drinkin' (With Lovin' on Your Mind)	1966
If You're Not Gone Too Long	1967
Fist City	1968
Your Squaw Is on the Warpath	1968
Coal Miner's Daughter	1969
Wings Upon Your Horns	1969
I Wanna Be Free	1970
You're Lookin' at Country	1970

ABOUT COUNTRY MUSIC
AND THE GRAND OLE OPRY

When Loretta Lynn first sang at the Grand Ole Opry in 1960, the Opry was already world famous. The Opry started in 1925 as a local Nashville radio program. It featured country bands and instrumentalists.

Crowds of people came to see the performers before and after the show. Finally the radio station built a special auditorium so the fans could watch the show. But the crowds kept growing and the Opry had to move to bigger and bigger places.

In 1938, the Opry first started featuring individual singers and groups. In 1939, the show was first carried nationally on NBC radio. Being heard across the country created more and more fans of the Opry and of country music.

This new national interest in country music made stars of many men and women in the Opry "family." Loretta mentions some of them in her book.

The late Ernest Tubb was important in Loretta's career. He put her on his radio program, which came on the air after the Opry show. They also made an album together. One of Tubb's best-remembered hits is "Walking the Floor over You."

Conway Twitty and Loretta were named the Top Vocal Duo of the Year in 1972. They have made many records together. Twitty is famous for composing "It's Only Make Believe" and "Hello Darlin'."

Kitty Wells, one of Loretta's idols, immortalized "Release Me" and "It Wasn't God Who Made Honky-Tonk Angels."

Speedy West, who helped Loretta with her first record, was named to the Country Music Hall of Fame in 1989.

Disc jockey and country musician Waylon Jennings also helped Loretta. He became famous for such songs as "Take It to the Limit" and "It's Only Rock and Roll."

Today Opryland has a 4,400-seat Opry House. Almost a million fans travel to Nashville every year to see the Friday, Saturday, and Sunday performances.

QUESTIONS FOR THE READER

Thinking about the Story

1. What did you think of the selections from *Coal Miner's Daughter*? What did you like or not like?

2. Are there ways that the events or people in the selections became important or special to you? Write about or discuss them.

3. What do you think were the most important things Loretta Lynn wanted to say in the selections?

4. In what ways did the selections answer the questions you had before you began reading or listening?

5. Were any parts of the selections difficult to understand? If so, you may want to read or listen to them again. You might think about why they were difficult.

Activities

1. Were there any words that were difficult for you in the selections from *Coal Miner's*

Daughter? Go back to these words and try to figure out their meanings. Discuss what you think each word means, and why you made that guess. Discuss with your teacher or another student how you are going to remember each word. Some ways to re-member words are to put them on file cards, or write them in your journal, or create a personal dictionary. Be sure to use the words in your writing in a way that will help you to remember the meaning.

2. How did you help yourself understand the selections? Did you ask yourself questions? What were they? Discuss these questions with other people who have read the same selections, or write about them in your journal.

3. Talking with other people about what you have read can increase your under-standing of it. Discussion can help you organize your thoughts, get new ideas, and rethink your original ideas. Discuss your thoughts about the selections with someone else who has read them. Find out if your opinions are the same or different. See if

your thoughts change as a result of this discussion.

4. After you finish reading or listening, you might want to write down your thoughts about *Coal Miner's Daughter*. You could write a book review, or a letter to a friend you think might be interested in Loretta Lynn. You could write your reflections on the book in your journal, or you could write about topics the book has brought up that you want to explore further.

5. Did reading the selections give you any ideas for your own writing? You might want to write about:

• one of your parents.

• the place where you grew up.

• an ambition you had and how you achieved it, or an ambition you have today and how you plan to achieve it.

6. Sometimes organizing information in a visual way can help you better understand or remember it. Look at the timeline for

Loretta Lynn on page 13. You might want to make a timeline of your own.

7. Loretta Lynn talks about some of the things that make country music special. You might want to write about the kind of music you like—for example, rock, gospel, jazz, classical—and what makes it special. You might want to make a tape of your favorite pieces of music and share it with some friends.

8. If you could talk to Loretta Lynn, what questions would you ask her? You might want to write the questions in your journal.

Seven series of good books for all readers:

WRITERS' VOICES
Selections from the works of America's finest and most popular writers, along with background information, maps, and other supplementary materials. Authors include: Kareem Abdul-Jabbar • Maya Angelou • Bill Cosby • Alex Haley • Stephen King • Loretta Lynn • Larry McMurtry • Amy Tan • Anne Tyler • Abigail Van Buren • Alice Walker • Tom Wolfe, and many others.

NEW WRITERS' VOICES
Anthologies and individual narratives by adult learners. A wide range of topics includes home and family, prison life, and meeting challenges. Many titles contain photographs or illustrations.

OURWORLD
Selections from the works of well-known science writers, along with related articles and illustrations. Authors include David Attenborough and Carl Sagan.

FOR YOUR INFORMATION
Clearly written and illustrated works on important self-help topics. Subjects include: Eating Right • Managing Stress • Getting Fit • About AIDS • Getting Good Health Care, among others.

TIMELESS TALES
Classic myths, legends, folk tales, and other stories from around the world, with special illustrations.

SPORTS
Fact-filled books on baseball, football, basketball, and boxing, with lots of action photos. With read-along tapes narrated by Phil Rizzuto, Frank Gifford, Dick Vitale, and Sean O'Grady.

SULLY GOMEZ MYSTERIES
Fast-paced detective series starring Sully Gomez and the streets of Los Angeles.

WRITE FOR OUR FREE COMPLETE CATALOG:

 SIGNAL HILL

Signal Hill Publications
P.O. Box 131
Syracuse, NY 13210-0131